THE MAGIC OF THE PYRAMIDS

— *and* —

THE MYSTERY OF THE SPHINX

A. BOTHWELL-GOSSE

E. Wedgwood

THE PYRAMIDS AT GIZEH

THE GREAT

The Magic of the Pyramids

and

The Mystery of the Sphinx

Tales and Traditions.

BY

A. BOTHWELL-GOSSE

AUTHOR OF

The Civilisation of the Ancient Egyptians,
The Knights Templars, etc.

LONDON
THEOSOPHICAL PUBLISHING SOCIETY
161, NEW BOND STREET, W.
1915

To

My Mother.

CONTENTS.

ERRATA.

Cover Design : *read* LIFE, STRENGTH, HEALTH.
Frontispiece : *reverse* The Light and The Supreme.

LIST OF ILLUSTRATIONS.

" Archæology . . . is garbed in an imperishable glamour, she is raised far above the turmoil of the present on the wings of Imagination. Her eyes are sombre with the memory of the wisdom driven from her scattered sanctuaries ; and at her lips wonderful things strive for utterance."

" The true lover of old and forgotten things . . . is a spectator of splendid pageants, a ministrant of strange rites, a witness to vast tragedies, he also has admittance to the magical kingdom, to which is added the freedom of the City of Remembrance."

BATTISCOMBE G. GUNN.

THE MAGIC OF THE PYRAMIDS

AND

THE MYSTERY OF THE SPHINX.

I.

THE PYRAMIDS.

I.

"A GREAT enchantment rests on this place from the beginning of time."

THE pyramids were an object of mysterious veneration even in the land of their origin.

Their antiquity, their immensity, their splendour, lent an imperishable glory, that radiating down the lingering centuries has endured with undiminished lustre until to-day.

Books innumerable have been written on the subject; the classic authors full of wonder and admiration extol the magnitude of these ancient works. Herodotus gives a strikingly accurate account of the dimensions and of the appearance in his day, which in exactness is only surpassed by Pliny. Diodorus Siculus presents a few more details, and Strabo adds an invaluable description of the entrance door to the great Pyramid. Later, the Arabs write glowing descriptions of their beauty, and dwell with enthusiasm on the ancient legends connected with them.   Modern writers next take up the tale and exercise their ingenuity in evolving theories, frequently quite untenable and inconsistent with the known facts and with the accurate measurements.

The etymology of the word "pyramid" is unknown.   It has come to us through the Greek πυραμίς, but its origin is disputed; it is not Greek and probably not Aryan and has no connection with πυρ flame or fire; derivation from sound alone is entirely misleading.   The word, like the object, is no doubt Egyptian, or as near to the Egyptian as the Greeks could manage, for they complained that they "could not get their tongue round the language"!   The Egyptian word Per-em-us ex-presses the idea* of "*height*" and as that is a notable characteristic of the pyramids (which at a distance look like mountains!) it is a reasonable derivation.

It was the custom to give special names to these monuments,—the Purest Place, the Rising of Souls, the Light, the Beautiful, the Southern, and so on. One goes by the name of the "Lying Pyramid"! The Arabs call it so, but whether, as is so frequently the case, they have adopted the ancient popular name,† is not now known.   It is very old, and was built at Medum, by Seneferu, who, with his wife Mertitefs, came to the throne in 4790 B.C.   This Pyramid no doubt earned its name from the fact

---

* Budge and Eisenlohr.
† Seneferu called it " The Rising," or " The Resurrection."

that it was not a pyramid at all, only an exalted mastaba,* masquerading as a pyramid, and was built in terraces. The terraces are all broken away giving it a tower-like appearance; an Arab author† says of this " Meidoun " pyramid, " it is like a mountain and has five terraces," but probably there were seven originally. Seneferu was not content with one pyramid but built another (calling it also " The Rising ") at Dahshur which is remarkable because it still shows traces of the pivot stone that closed the entrance, and within which was a wooden door. It is well known that the pyramids were entered by a revolving stone, but this is now the only one where the mechanism can be traced.

This pyramid has two entrances, one on the north and one on the west. An ancient Coptic tradition has it that one of the pyramids "at Dahsoor was built before the flood " by a king who possessed profound knowledge of chemistry. He safeguarded his eternal resting-place by creating " speaking images " which occupied the pyramid, and the outside was guarded by spirits who appeared in the form of two old black men. There are several pyramids in the neighbourhood in various states of disrepair but to which of all of them this legend belongs, it is difficult now to tell.

No doubt Seneferu was a great and glorious King but it is his fate to be overshadowed by a famous

---

* A mastaba has an angle of about 76°, and a rise of 4 on base of 1. A pyramid has an angle of about 52°, and a rise of 14 on base of 11.

† Makrisi, cir. 1400, A.D.

magician and to be remembered chiefly by a story recounting the exploits of this marvellous man! Seneferu, depressed by the cares of government, and by the famine and the invasion that had occurred in his reign, sank into melancholy from which Mertitefs and the courtiers failed to rouse him.

Zazamankh the magician proposed a pleasure trip by boat, so that his mind should be weaned from these depressing matters and "his heart might be expanded" by the sunshine, the fresh air, and the beauty of the scene :—a special point was made of this last! To ensure variety too, the rowers chosen for the boat were twenty of the most beautiful maidens of the court, clothed in garments of "network" adorned with jewels, and provided with paddles of exquisite workmanship, ebony inlaid with gold! So they set forth on the still waters of the lake, and midway the "mafkhet" * jewel worn by one of the maidens, being loosened no doubt by the exertion of rowing, fell into the water, which was more than twenty feet deep at this part. Confusion followed, the maiden cried out in distress and the rowing stopped. The King endeavoured to pacify her and promised to give her another turquoise even of greater value, but she refused to be comforted and reiterated that she preferred her own and wanted it back again. Zazamankh then took the matter in hand! He rose up and recited spells and incantations over the

* A blue or green stone, probably turquoise or malachite or, less likely, emerald.

lake, whereupon the waters receded* and piled themselves up, forty feet on either side, revealing the bottom with the mafkhet jewel lying in full view.

From thence it was rescued and returned to its delighted owner. The magician, by again exercising his magic powers, then restored the piled-up waters to their place, and the lake was as before, a calm unruffled surface. • Such a marvellous episode, occurring on such a romantic expedition, could not fail to rouse any King from a state of mental depression!

Seneferu had no monopoly either of magic or of pyramids, and his son who succeeded him outshone his achievements in both!

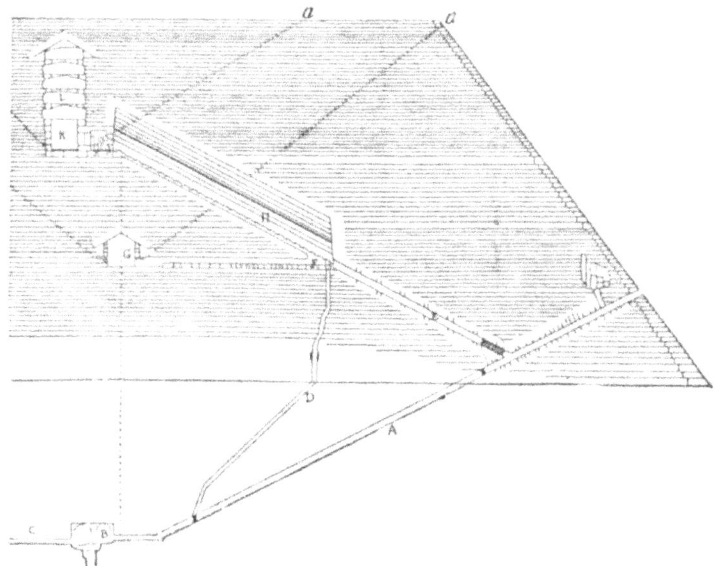

PASSAGES AND CHAMBERS IN "THE LIGHT."

* Moses emulated this feat a couple of thousand years later.

2.

" THE LIGHT."

" THE maritime pyramid was a temple of the stars and in it there was a figure of the sun and moon both of which spoke."

MURTADA.

SENEFERU having departed this life, Khufu reigned in his stead.

His pyramid, which we are accustomed to call the Great, he called the Light or the Glory and it far surpassed all others in size, in wonders and in legendary lore. Except a few very modern slender towers no building equals it in height, which originally was 481 feet* although now, owing to destruction it is 30 feet less.   It is 756 feet square, covering 13½ acres, and is said to contain 89 million cubic feet of stone.   But these are words and convey no sense of its vastness to the mind, some idea, however, of this immensity may be gained from the fact, that Howard Vyse spent £10,000 on excavations merely in order to measure it, and there is an Arab tale of an old king, who calculated that all the wealth in Egypt in his time would not enable him to destroy the pyramid !   It is oriented† to the cardinal points of

---

* Professor Petrie's measurements are used throughout this chapter, reduced to feet and omitting the decimals.

† It is *now* 4′ W. of N., astronomers state that there is a variation of position of the Pole, amounting to about 1′ in a 1,000 years so the presumption is that the orientation was absolutely correct when the pyramid was built.

THE LIGHT

E. Wedgwood

heaven and the entrance is in the North face about 24 feet East of the centre and 55 feet above the original pavement. It was closed by a self-replacing stone swinging on a horizontal hinge; when this was in place the entrance was invisible and there was nothing to distinguish it from the other casing-stones. The secret was known to the Roman officials and is described* thus:—“It has on its side, at a moderate elevation, a stone which can be moved. When it has been lifted up, a sloping passage is seen.”

After the Roman occupation the knowledge was lost, and so perfectly was the doorway concealed that once lost it could not be discovered !

The destruction of the pyramid began in the early years of the ninth century, when the Kaliph al Mamun ruthlessly quarried into the masonry to find some mode of ingress. For his operations he chose the centre of the North face and naturally missed the passage which lay above and to the East. After making a gigantic cavity (known to this day as Mamun’s Hole), the excavators heard “ a great stone fall into a hollow space,” dislodged doubtless by the vigour of their blows. Guessing that accident had now revealed that for which they had sought in vain for many months, they turned their work towards the sound in “ the hollow space ” and burst presently into the passage—the passage that ran from the entrance downwards to the subterranean regions. But it also shewed them *another* passage sloping upwards which had been

* Strabo.

hidden by the stone that fell, and of which the Romans knew nothing—in fact it might never have been revealed up to this day, had not the tremendous vibrations dislodged it !

In the downward passage the first unexplained object is met with, a large granite block,* partly dressed and partly rough, with a portion of a 4-inch drill hole, running through the entire thickness, on one side. Where this came from and what its original use cannot *even* be surmised. The masonry round about is limestone, there is granite however in the ascending passage, and this stone may possibly be the "great stone which fell into a hollow space" and which originally closed that passage. The only other possible place is the Antechamber, and Maillet speaks of a block lying there that is certainly not there now—but it was 6 feet by 4 feet, much larger than this one.

The passage runs down for about 300 feet passing through the masonry and then the solid rock ; at this level it turns horizontally, opens out into a side chamber, and finally terminates in a large vault, which lies South of the main axis of the pyramid. This chamber has never been finished ; huge masses of rock, unexcavated, rise from the floor to within ten inches of the roof in some places. Skirting round this chaos, a strange shaft, descending vertically through the rock, is found ; also another passage goes further south, and ends abruptly.

---

* This stone is 45in. by 32in. by 20½in., the faces and one end are dressed, the sides and other end are rough broken ; the drill hole is 27.3in. from the worked end.

Along two sides of this shaft, nearly 6 feet down, is a broad ledge, beyond which there is a further descent of more than 3 feet.

The purpose of these mysterious rock-hewn sub-terranean passages, vaults, and shafts, has never been solved, so we fall back on Pliny*: “In the interior of the largest Pyramid there is a well 86 cubits deep, which communicates with the river it is thought.”

The depth does not seem right, but there are other traditions of a communication with the Nile, and the cutting of this underground water channel is mentioned as one of the excessive hardships imposed on the labourers by the builder.

Returning from these underground regions we reach the junction with the ascending passage. Here is a yawning gulf, as so much of the masonry has been destroyed by Mamun's Arabs! This devastating horde, finding the upper passage plugged with huge granite blocks, bored a way through the softer limestone core-masonry, keeping alongside them, until, getting past the end of the obstacle, they could enter the passage itself.

This passage is of practical masonic interest; the roof and sides of the part that is plugged, are in one piece, *i.e.*, they are girdle blocks; the passage narrows slightly towards the blocked exit, and the plugs taper to fit the narrowing; in this way, both the sliding downward of the plugs was prevented, and the outward thrust of the weight, was equalised.

* Pliny XXXVI., 16., 17.

Just beyond these blocks there are two horizontal joints in the roof, which is inconveniently low. At one time it was thought that these joints marked the beginning of another concealed passage, but, as the stones are also girdle blocks, the idea seems quite untenable.

Next, a level landing-place is reached, and on the West is the head of the shaft that descends* into the subterranean passages, this must have been closed originally to permit of the passage of the plug blocks; the exit also must have been concealed as the Romans apparently did not know of its existence.

This shaft was undoubtedly sunk after the pyramid core was built, because the first part of it was cut through the masonry. The remainder, which is precipitous, goes through the solid rock; one part of this has been called " the Grotto," and here again a secret passage was sought for, but it turned out to be only a waterworn fissure in the rock that had been built over, to shore up the loose gravel.

From the landing place a horizontal passage leads to the Queen's Chamber†, it runs immediately under the gallery floor, and therefore must have been completely hidden when the sloping floor of the gallery and passage was an unbroken incline. The chamber is of granite and obtains its name from the gable form of the roof. Among the Arabs a man's tomb has a flat roof, whereas a woman's has a sloping roof; noticing these peculiarities the

* More than 140 feet.

† The Dimensions of the Queen's Chamber are about 18ft. long by 17ft. wide by 15ft. high, but 20ft. high at the ridge.

Arabs called the two principal rooms, the King's and Queen's Chambers respectively.

The ridge of the gable-roof is exactly in the plane of the central axis of the pyramid.

The Arab historians say that an empty sarcophagus stood . in this chamber in their day, this has now disappeared !

Another enigma presents itself in the two so-called air channels leading to this Chamber. Now, until they were ruthlessly broken through, these were closed by a plate of stone where they should have emerged, therefore certainly no air could ever have reached the room through them. Is it at all likely that this was merely an omission on the part of the builders ? Or was the original purpose quite otherwise ? They were undoubtedly useless for ventilation, indeed it is not even known whether they penetrated to the outside at all ! Is it possible that these passages were connected with the acoustic properties of the Chamber ?

There is evidence shewing that this suggestion is at least possible, for a party of explorers who were in the highest construction chamber, found they could hear *distinctly* the men who were working at the mouth of the southern air channel to the King's Chamber.

In the Eastern wall there is a niche 41 inches, deep as if designed for a statue, and, under the floor near it there is a cavity about 4 feet deep; there is an old tradition that an “idol” occupied the niche; undoubtedly there are quantities of pieces of diorite, wrought and polished, outside the pyramid, opposite the entrance, which suggest that some diorite object was there smashed to pieces.

The "idol," perhaps, was the image of the King's Ka, worshipped after his death, and exercising strange powers that gave rise to stories of mysterious hauntings. "A great enchantment rests on this place from the beginning of time," was the expressed opinion of the Egyptians themselves thousands of years ago. That opinion was shared by the Arabs, who believed that each pyramid had such a magic guardian to protect it, and who even to-day narrate strange tales of the weird entities who guard the pyramids.

"In the great Pyramid was an image of black agate, with eyes open and shining, sitting on a throne, with a kingly sceptre. When any man looked on this statue, he heard on one side of him a voice, which took away his senses, and he who heard that voice died." This is so suggestive of a black diorite statue with inlaid eyes which may have occupied the niche in the Queen's Chamber, that perhaps the account is not wholly due to the exuberant oriental imagination; and the strange channels that were in the side walls of the room and the useless cavity in the floor, also recur to the mind in connection with this story of the terrible sound that killed! And the natural speculation arises, as to what part absolute terror of the unknown, may have played in the smashing to atoms of such a statue!

This idea is indirectly confirmed by Herodotus, who mentions the insuperable dislike shewn by the

Egyptians to pronouncing the *name* of the builders of the pyramids, and imputes it to hatred, but there can be no doubt that the real root of the instinctive objection to "naming a Name," is fear.

To the Egyptians there was great significance in a name; the name gave actual existence, the sound produced, or called into being, it endowed an object with life, and this could only be got rid of by destroying or breaking the object. The potency lay in the name, it was indeed a thing to conjure with, a magic spell, a mantram!

Returning from the Queen's Chamber to the landing-place, the ascending passage now becomes the Grand Gallery*.

This is of polished limestone and shows great constructive ability. Its roof is lofty, and the stones forming it are so placed that the pressure which otherwise would cause the whole roof to slide down the incline, is transferred to the walls. The last seven courses of stone, in the upper part of the walls, are so built that each projects over the one below, thus lessening the width of the gallery, until finally, the width of the roof equals the width of the floor space. The third lap has a groove running its entire length; its meaning is unknown. Its position is midway between the floor and roof, and from the direction of the tool-marks, the line was drawn after the stones were *in situ*. The grooves are opposite each other, and suggest that something

* About 148 feet long and 28 high.

was laid across, dividing the gallery into two stories as it were ; two galleries each 14 feet in height. The depth of the groove, rather more than $\frac{3}{4}$ of an inch, would support short lengths of wood, and the fact that the upper edge is slightly cut away, would facilitate the laying of the planks in position.

Of course this is mere conjecture, but it has two points in its favour, it provides a *raison d'être* for the grooves ; and, such an upper gallery would render more accessible the entrance to the room above the King's Chamber. Without this supposition one cannot conceive how it was reached, as it is situated at the top of the eastern wall 28 feet above the present floor !

No trace of any wood remains, but that need cause no surprise, for apart from the destructive action of immense periods of time, the Egyptians used rare and costly woods, inlaid and carved. A tessellated pavement of ebony and ivory, or of cedar, would have been rapidly removed by the plundering hordes that, from time to time, burst into the royal tombs, removing everything of value.

Running the entire length of each side of the gallery is a raised stone platform, these are generally called 'ramps.' They are almost 2 feet high, and about 20 inches wide. Each ramp has twenty-eight holes drilled in it, these are alternately long and short, and above each hole is a grooved block in the wall. No reasonable suggestion has ever been offered as to the purpose of these holes and grooves. May they not have afforded support for the flooring suggested above or for the fittings of some lighting apparatus to illuminate this magnificent gallery?

The central axis of the pyramid passes through the south end, and there at the head of the gallery, is a large stone. It has been called a step, a dais or a throne. As it is more than 6 feet long and nearly 3 feet high the word "step" does not seem appropriate. The ramps practically touch it at each side, therefore, if they were used as benches, this block being rather higher, might be called a dais or a throne. No one has suggested that it might be an altar stone but that idea seems as likely as any of the others. The one undoubted point about it, is, that it accurately marks the transition from the Northern to the Southern half of the pyramid. Climbing over this block (there is not much room, only 42 inches!) the horizontal passage is reached which soon widens out into the Ante-Chamber. The walls here are exceedingly rough, contrasting in a marked manner with the exquisite polish of the Grand Gallery. There is a high and thick granite wainscot in which grooves are cut at intervals, and in one set of these grooves, just within the room, is a granite portcullis about 4 feet wide and the same in height, extending right across the room in mid-air. Further progress is impossible without either crawling under or climbing over this obstacle.* This is the most puzzling room in the pyramid! Why is the wainscot a foot higher on the West side than on the East? And what is the meaning of the three

* There is a space of $3\frac{3}{8}$ feet below and $4\frac{3}{4}$ feet above.

GROOVES AND SEMICIRCULAR CUP-SHAPED HOLLOWS
IN WEST WAINSCOT.

unused grooves? These three grooves have cup-shaped hollows at the top. In addition there are four grooves in the South wall above the entrance to the King's Chamber. Everything is suggestive of fittings* of some kind. Perhaps this was the mechanical chamber containing the apparatus for manipulating the heavy movable stone doors. Three, and possibly four of these existed; the revolving stone pivot of the portal, the traps at the head and exit of the well-shaft, and the entrance to the Queen's passage and Chamber. The grooves and cup hollows seem just adapted for the pillars in the Coptic tradition.

"Within the great Pyramid are three marble columns supporting the images of three birds in

---

* The granite is daubed over with cement in many places.

flames of fire. Upon the first was that of a dove, formed of a green stone ; upon the second that of a hawk of yellow stone ; and upon the third that of a cock of red stone. Upon moving the hawk a door composed of great marble slabs, beautifully put together, and inscribed with unknown characters, was raised ; and the same connection existed between the other images and their doors " !

The birds were evidently the handles of levers that altered the compensating weights. Some such arrangement must have existed, for the pivot door-stone required a pull of 4cwt. upwards, to raise it sufficiently to pass into the passage with ease, and no doubt the other doors were equally heavy.

A short low passage* proceeds to the King's Chamber. An earthquake has caused much damage here, everyone of the massive roof beams are fractured and the joints have started. This room† is of polished granite, except the roof, which is flat and weighs about 400 tons, and which has been left rough dressed. It contains a large plain sarco-phagus‡ of red granite, and far from being highly polished it bears the marks of the saw and of a tube drill ! These flaws in the workmanship are infinitely more instructive than the perfections which only excite our admiration. Professor Petrie considers that a bronze saw, about 9 feet long, with jewelled points, must have been used by the masons in

* The passage is about 8ft. long, 3½ high and the same in width.

† 34ft. by 17ft. by 19ft.

‡ Inside, roughly 6½ft. by 2·3ft. by 2·10ft. Outside 7·6ft. by 3ft. by 3·6ft.

cutting off this slice of granite nearly 8 feet long. The saw went a fraction too deep and had to be backed out; in like manner, in the inside, the tube drill got off the vertical—these two flaws the ancient masons tried to obliterate by polishing, but fortunately the errors remain patent, demonstrating their methods to us of modern times. Originally there was a fitted lid, for there is an under-cut groove to fix it and three pin-holes to hold the bronze pins.

The chamber is ventilated by two air channels now choked with wind-borne sand. In one of them was found a piece of iron, and it is now conceded that this iron is contemporary with the building of the pyramid. There is a cast of a nummulite on the rust, proving that it lay buried for ages pressed upon by the nummulitic limestone.

Among the wonderful treasures mentioned by the Arab historians, as being stored away in the pyramids was " precious iron that would twine about like cloth." They mention iron too as being used for securing the drums of pillars. This find proves the correctness of their accounts of the early use of this metal.

Above the King's Chamber are the five " Construction Chambers," one above the other. Their purpose is to support the colossal weight of the super-imposed mass and to prevent it crushing the roof of the King's Chamber. The first is entered by a short passage* from the roof of the Grand

* Twenty feet.

Gallery, no entrance has been found to the upper four, but they are reached through the shaft cut directly upwards by Howard Vyse. The roof of each chamber forms the floor of the next above, and is made of long granite blocks which are rough dressed on the lower face that forms the ceiling, and very rough " ashlar " work on the upper face which forms the floor of the storey above.

Masons' marks abound in these chambers, some are masons' marks made in the quarries or stone yards, others are builders' marks indicating the exact position for erection. Each roof beam has a central and two end lines and they are *all numbered*. There are also lines for " dressing " the stone level when in place. Some have been drawn during the process of building as they are visible not only under the plaster but *over* it. The lines are in both red and black paint, the black ones being apparently the final correction, and they are both horizontal and vertical; in the highest chamber these lines have triangles on them, in one case there is a large red triangle containing a small black one. In addition to the marks there are hieroglyphics, some drawn after the stones were in place because they pass over the joint from one stone to another; others again were drawn in the stoneyard or in the quarry and are now upside down !

All arrangements, even in detail, were therefore made in the quarries or stone-yards so that the erection could proceed quickly and smoothly with the material which had been not only prepared, but *fitted* according to the architect's plan. These minute directions remind us of the commands laid upon the builders of another famous structure, more than 2000 years later, the Temple of Solomon the King, "built of stone made ready before it was brought thither : so that there was neither hammer nor axe nor any tool of iron heard in the house while it was in building."*

Having finished the examination of the inside of the pyramid and weighing carefully all the measurements and comparing them, the well marked limits of size necessitate certain definite conclusions. For instance the sarcophagus must have been placed in the King's Chamber during the process of erection, as it is an inch wider than the beginning of the ascending passage! Also the size of the plug blocks compels the verdict, that before they were slid down to their final position to close the passage against intruders, they must have occupied the floor of the gallery between the ramps. They are too large to occupy the passage to the Queen's Chamber and the mouth of the Well is so small as to entirely negative the possibility of their being stored elsewhere and then fetched up the shaft when wanted. But if they occupied the Grand Gallery the way to the King's Chamber must have been exceedingly awkward, and anyone entering must perforce have climbed over the blocks or walked up the ramps.

When the time came to move them to the intended place, the entrance to the Queen's Chamber must have been closed so that the floorway should

* I. Kings vi., 7.

be continuous. They were then slid down, and there they are to this day!

The chambers and passages of the pyramid take up a comparatively small area, in fact, so minute a proportion, that others may still be concealed within its vast dimensions. The ancients always use the plural in speaking of the underground chambers, and the tomb is stated to have been on an island in the centre, but the one underground chamber known is nowhere near the centre, and is a chaos of rock.

It is true the so-called Queen's Chamber is cut by the midplane, but the dead centre is exactly where the two axes cross, many feet west of this chamber; and moreover the Queen's Chamber is neither underground, nor is it an island. From this we may infer that discoveries may yet be made.

That there is still a mysterious and unknown entrance may be gathered from the fact that a large round- flint pebble was found* under the coffer in the King's Chamber. *How* did the man, who tilted up the sarcophagus with a desert pebble, gain access to the chamber? That remains an unsolved problem! The deed was done before the entrances had been all smashed up and broken open, because then, the floors, the passages, and chambers were literally smothered with broken stones of all sizes and a piece would have been selected from the *débris!* The interior must have been clean, swept and garnished to render it necessary to fetch a stone from the desert to prop up the coffer! And yet,

---

* Professor Petrie gives an interesting acccunt of this pebble.

admittance to all the upper part was impossible by the closing and concealing of the means of ingress from the main passage! If the plates of stone covering the ingress and egress to and from the Well shaft were hinged, or revolving, then this man must have been at home in the passages and chambers, and acquainted with the " open sesame " that moved the stones. If however, they were cemented into place, then the conclusion is inevitable ; there must be another secret entrance available to those who knew.

A tradition of a subterranean passage existed in remote times. Strange stories are told about people getting into it accidently and emerging outside the pyramid.

About twenty young men taking food, crowbars, other tools and lanterns set out to explore all the passages, chambers and crypts. Most of them got down " from the first descent and the second and passed along the ground of the pyramid . . ." till they came to a narrow passage through which came an " impetuous wind and extraordinary cold." They went in but the place seemed " joyned and close before them so a rope was tied round the waist of one and he entered " but the passage closed in upon him and they could not get him back when they hauled in the rope. " A dreadful voice came out of the cave startling them and they fell down." When they became conscious again they with difficulty found their way out. Sitting down to rest and consider all that had befallen them their companion suddenly rose out of the earth before them, he remained as if dead for two hours then he spoke in an unknown tongue and died !

Another party descended to the lowest part and “ turned round about ” ; seeing a hollow place where there was a beaten path they proceeded until they came to a fountain of fresh water, thence to a square hall the walls of which were of strange coloured stones. Cisterns of gold next attracted their attention and wonderful mechanical statues of cocks that crowed, and lions that roared. There was also a tall ancient man of green stone and many other marvels, but “ commending themselves to God they kept on their way ” till at last they saw a light and going towards it they found themselves in the “ great sandy desert.” This passage was guarded by two statues of black stone. They then returned Eastwards towards the pyramids.

These stories were well known, so in very early times great excavations were made beyond the pyramid, to search for the subterranean entrance. On the north side a deep hollow filled with stones and chips was found under the pavement. It was cleared out again by Vyse to the depth of 45 feet and found to extend to within 10 feet of the structure ; a grotto and channel branched from it. He concluded that it was a natural cleft in the rock and as further work was difficult owing to the narrowness, nothing more was done.

The Arab historians say that the “ gate ” of this pyramid is “ on the south side 100 cubits distant from the western wall ”—the only entrance that *we* know is on the north !

The immensity of this monument impresses the senses, the beauty of workmanship excites the admiration and the extraordinary skill of construction astonishes the intellect. The accuracy and trueness of the squaring of the huge blocks of stone is compared by Professor Petrie to "the finest optician's work but on a scale of acres instead of feet." The outside, of white limestone, was so highly polished that it looked like one immense slab, glittering, and reflecting the brilliant Egyptian sun, thereby justifying its ancient name of "the Glory" or "the Light." Many of these casing stones weighed about 16 tons and yet a tissue-paper-like layer of cement was spread between each, and they were so exquisitely fitted that no join was visible ; so perfectly indeed, that as we have seen, the position of the pivot door-stone was lost !

The workmanship of the entrance passage and Queen's Chamber is just as wonderful, but higher up the floors are out of level, much of the granite has never been dressed, the knobs for lifting the stones into position have not been removed and the part levelled and polished like the rest of the surface, as was the general custom. The separating of the joints and the upper floors being out of level, are certainly attributable to earthquakes, but the other points are distinct flaws in the character of the building, and there is evidence of carelessness, hurry, and bad work. The variation in the style of the building is so striking that Professor Petrie suggests it may be "owing to the death of the man who had really directed the superfine accuracy of the earlier work." This would explain the deterioration. Moreover it is an interesting idea and reminds us of a legend of another country and another age, which relates the story of the death of the principal architect, just before the completion of the temple. A loss so important could not but be speedily felt, and the work fell into temporary confusion owing to the loss of the plans which had been regularly supplied till then to every department.

It is always difficult to trace the origin of traditions. Perhaps this one arose in Egypt during the erection of the pyramid? The Acacia which plays a prominent part in the story grows abundantly in Egypt and is there a sacred plant.

The theories founded on the dimensions of the pyramid are endless, for the subject excites the imagination and stimulates the mind. Most of them however are untenable because they are not in accordance with fact. Professor Petrie's splendid work and brilliant deductions have · cleared the ground, and although many of these beliefs must now be given up, other definite knowledge has been established on a secure foundation. There can be no doubt that the pyramid was constructed to an architectural plan, and is not a fortuitous collection of stories added from year to year. This original plan was carried out with an amazing skill that has never been equalled. The dimensions express certain geometrical truths, such as the famous proposition of Euclid demonstrating the relation which the hypotenuse bears to the sides of a right-angled triangle. This was one of the most cherished secrets of the mediæval masons of Europe. The angle of construction shews that the ancient Egyptian architect understood the exact relation between the diameter and the circumference of a circle.

But not only is mathematical skill displayed, astronomical knowledge is also expressed. Here again however some favourite ideas must be relinquished. It is oriented to the cardinal points, but the entrance tunnel could not have been directed to α Draconis as the dates do not agree. The pyramid must certainly have been built at least 1700 years before the epoch in which this star became the Pole Star. Outside the pyramid, beyond the beautiful white limestone pavement that originally surrounded it, are three deep trenches just such as could have been used for the stellar observations which were certainly taken. Filled with water and with cord stretched across, the transit of the reflection of a star over the cord could be noted and the observations recorded. The Egyptians had books treating of the positions of the fixed stars, and their observations of total eclipses of the sun and moon went back for about 20,000 years. The Arabs have many tales of the star observations taken here.

The most fascinating of the many theories is that of Marsham Adams, who considers that this stupendous building illustrates in stone what the *Book of the Dead* teaches in words: that the pyramid was, in fact, a Temple of Initiation where the soul, freed from the body, passed through successive portals. After many mystic journeys it was made free of various planes, and became endowed with powers won by conquest over its lower self manifesting as entities of those planes. Progressing through one initation after another the postulant sounds the secrets of both Life and Death and "passing through the hidden place penetrates the secret of the House of Light."

Anyone well acquainted with this wonderful Egyptian Scripture will be struck by the extra-ordinary way the words and scenes correspond with the points in the interior of the pyramid.

Most historians, ancient and modern, state that the Great Pyramid was built by Khufu* miscalled Kheops by the Greeks. Notwithstanding this there is a difference of opinion among the Greek and Arab authors and some uncertainty is introduced by the fact that the blocks of stone within the pyramid bear two names, Khufu and Khnum Khuf. Some authorities think that they co-operated in the building of the pyramid, in that case Khnum Khuf was the more important as his name comes first. No king of that name is known nor is the name found except in connection with quarrying for the stone and within the building itself. Also he must have died first, as Khufu's name is found very frequently alone. It may be that one of these great men built, and the other either repaired or completed the monument. It has been pointed out that there was a change of plan in the construction, or that extensive alterations were carried out after the building was completed; such are, the grooving of the walls in the Grand Gallery and the insertion of

* Khufu was the second king of Dynasty IV., about 4,700 B.C.

the grooved blocks in the wall behind the ramps; also, the well-shaft was undoubtedly dug out through masonry previously built. In the King's Chamber one of the roof-beams which had been fractured by an earthquake was plastered over to mend the flaw— here is definite evidence of repair.

Confirming this idea of two distinct personalities are the traditions that exist concerning the builder. These are so contradictory and so diametrically opposed that they can only be reconciled by the thought that they were based on the memories of two very different men, connected through their operations on the pyramid in the minds of the people, and confused together owing to the resemblance of the names.

One tradition narrates how Khufu was loved by his people who under his beneficent reign were prosperous and happy, and "having written a sacred book he was translated to the gods." "The just of speech" he is called in a medical work. This book was revealed to a priest of Isis at Coptos during a midnight vigil. "Although the earth was plunged into darkness, the moon shone upon it and enveloped it with light. It was sent as a great wonder to his holiness the King, Khufu, the just of speech." As well as the sacred book and the medical work, two treatises on alchemy are ascribed to him. Manetho is in agreement as to his literary capacity, also saying that "he wrote the sacred book which is regarded by the Egyptians as a work of great importance" but he adds "he was arrogant towards the gods." Herodotus goes further and says that on coming to the throne "he plunged into every kind of wickedness and shut up all the Temples"—the people writhed under his oppression and his conduct caused him to be execrated by the multitude.

The manner of his death and burial varies as much as the accounts of his character. In one apparently he did not die at all but ascended into heaven. Another account* tells us that the people revolting against his infamous rule threatened to " drag his carcase out of the grave and tear it piecemeal " so when he died he was hurriedly buried in secret in an unknown place. Against this, is the persistent tradition that he was buried in an island under the centre of the pyramid, surrounded by a channel supplied with water from the Nile.

Surely these contradictions justify the assumption that they allude to different people of a like name. No one can doubt that *some* illustrious king found here his eternal resting-place, for Al Mamun's Arabs discovered within the pyramid a "stone coffer in which lay a case of green stone in the form of a man. In the green case was a human body clad in armour of gold adorned with precious stones, beside him was a sword of inestimable value and an emerald vase, above his head a ruby as large as an egg and brilliant as the sun, having characters which no man can read." Was this Khufu or Khnum Khuf? No one can now say. If however the island story is true then it may have been the latter. It is certainly curious and interesting that an island

* Diodorus Siculus,

tomb *has* been found not far from here. It belongs
to this era, and there is a moat round it. In the
course of centuries it had been demolished and
subsequently it had again been used as a burying
place. Within it a gold ring was found bearing the
cartouche of Khufu ! Professor Petrie considers that
this ring belonged to a priest of the great king,
buried here in later times. On the ground above it
there is now nothing, but some superstructure
originally existed, no doubt a shrine or chapel
dedicated to the worship of the revered dead. Was
this perhaps " the secret place " to which the body
of the great king was borne by stealth at night, by
a few faithful and devoted servants lest the enraged
multitude should revenge themselves by rending
the limbs in pieces and scattering them to the winds
of heaven ?

East of the Great Pyramid is a splendid basalt
pavement, all that now remains of some large
structure, of great magnificence judging by the
quantity of rare polished stones lying amid the
rubbish. It could scarcely be anything else but
the Pyramid Temple. Hereabout too are many
passages cut in the rock. Some are apparently an
experimental diagram of the interior passages of the
pyramid ; others are narrow deep trenches for astronomical observation and a few again are obviously
for drainage.

Another feature of interest in the neighbourhood
is the artificial extension of the plateau to the North
and South. The builders' rubbish was here tipped
over the cliff and the amount was so great that about

300 feet has thus been added to the original surface. The rubbish has been examined by sinking trenches and pits; it consists of masons' waste, cut chips, workman's broken eathernware crocks, charcoal, etc. ; in amount, in nature of material, and in the apparent age of the same, it appears to be from the Great Pyramid. Of course there have been other great buildings near by, but if this builders' "tip" is really the waste accumulation of the Great Pyramid, the theory that it was built before the "Flood" must be given up. That however is the Coptic tradition, mentioned by many historians with slightly varying detail.

Would builders' "tip" survive any flood, and continue stratified just as tossed over, like this has remained even until to-day? There is some doubt however whether the antediluvian pyramids were those at Gizeh. One MS. says they were in the neighbourhood of Syene, and another mentions Dahshoor, but all are agreed that "the reason for building the pyramids was because of the dream that Saurid the son of Sahaloc saw." This was, that the world was to be destroyed by water and then by fire, so he commanded that the pyramids should be built to ensure the safety of marvellous treasure and also to preserve all the knowledge of the arts and sciences. He then appointed magic guardians and made "exquisite talismans," and spirits to serve each guardian "which never went from before it." In addition he caused the place to be haunted by living spirits and special offerings and sacrifices belonged to them. The Great Pyramid was haunted by a "beardless

youth with a green skin and large teeth." After the
Deluge Mazar reigned in Egpyt, and the High Priest
Philemon opened the pyramids; together they took
out all the treasure and recovered the lost knowledge
of the world.

From Maspero.]

KHUFU.

E. Wedgwood

THE GREAT

3.

"THE GREAT."

"AND here were buried exquisite talismans of sapphire and symbols of emerald and images made with the substance of the stars."

COPTIC TRADITION.

KHUFU having passed to the realm of Osiris, Khafra reigned in his stead.

His pyramid is called "the Great"; in spite of its ambitious title it is much smaller* than the one we are accustomed to call by that name, and it was placed further South and West, but on the same plateau as his father's.† There are several interesting differences in the construction shewing that the architect was by no means a slavish imitator, but was possessed of originality; also, he anticipated that spirit of modernity which says "what the eye doth not see, the heart doth not grieve for," consequently the building is a strange mixture of perfection and slovenliness. Everything, inside and out, that can be seen is perfect, but the core-masonry and all that is hidden, is bad in every way!

It is oriented to the North and the entrance lies East of the centre. The passage slopes down and is

---

* Height 472ft., length of side 706ft. 2in.

† Or brother's.

first of built masonry, then it is cut in the rock; it afterwards runs horizontally and terminates in a formidable granite portcullis, sliding in grooves. This has been raised up, so by crawling under it access is gained to a further and loftier length of passage which leads to the sepulchral chamber.* This is entirely excavated out of the solid rock and has a gable roof of limestone; the pavement is limestone and granite, and the walls are stuccoed. The granite sarcophagus† far surpasses in beauty of workmanship and exquisite polish that in the King's Chamber of the Great Pyramid. It is entirely sunk into the floor and its lid is lying beside it, wrenched off by insatiable robbers, who, seeking for jewels and gold, did not scruple to lay sacrilegious hands on the royal mummies.

Returning from this rifled tomb we perceive, in the floor of the horizontal part of the passage, the mouth of another passage sloping downwards to the North. Following this, the direction presently becomes horizontal and widens out on the East into a recess, opposite which is the entrance to a short sloping passage, directly at right angles to it, terminating in a large vault.‡ The recess is obviously an enlargement for turning the sarcophagus to get it round the awkward right-angled passage, whereas in the upper chamber the coffer must have been placed in position during the

---

* Rather more than 46ft. by 16 by 17ft. high.

† Rather more than 8.7ft. by 3.5ft. by 3.2ft. deep outside and 7ft. by 2.2ft. by 2.5ft. inside.

‡ 34ft by 10ft.

erection of the pyramid and before the roof was put on, because it is an inch wider than all the passages! Departing from this subterranean chamber it is unnecessary to return to the main passage, for this one begins to ascend and finds an exit outside the pyramid in the pavement, about 40 feet from the base. This, which is really another entrance, forms the basis for the suggestion that there may be in like manner another entrance to the Great Pyramid from the pavement beyond it.

As before remarked, the only entrances that have been discovered are on the North face in both pyramids but one legend says that the gate of the oriental pyramid faces the East to see the rising sun, that of the occidental pyramid is at the West to see the sun set and that of the southern pyramid on the South to mark the sun at its meridian.

But to return to this second unexpected passage! Another gigantic portcullis closes this exit to intruders. This particular stone affords positive proof that the Egyptians had some mechanical device for moving heavy weights when human traction was impossible. This granite block weighs about two tons; and, it has been estimated, would require more than forty men to lift it. Owing to the size of the passage, not more than half a dozen at the very most, could be lifting and hauling on the stone—and yet it was introduced into the passage, turned round and fitted into the grooves! The secret method, whereby this race manipulated vast masses of extraordinary weight has not transpired, but the results justify the supposition that they possessed marvellous knowledge and skill long since forgotten.

This pyramid was also cased with polished lime-stone but the two lowest courses were of red granite. On the top of it, the Arabs say, there used to be a golden statue 40 cubits high, carved so magnificently that the features could be distinguished on the Mokattam Mountains nine miles off. Some authorities have thought that all the pyramids that terminated in a platform were adorned with the statue of the King who lay beneath.

A wall at least 20 feet high surrounds three sides of it. Beyond this wall on the West are many galleries, the masons' barracks, providing accommodation for about 4000 men. The stoneyards were there also, and the sculptors apparently had their workshops there too, as many pieces of statuary lie about. The estimate of the number of men is by no means excessive when the size of the pyramids is realised. Herodotus tells us that it took twenty years to build the Great Pyramid so there must have been a permanent colony of workmen in the neighbourhood. He also adds that 100,000 worked at a time "each party during three months." These were used for traction and for making the great causeway from the quarries, also for excavating the underground chambers in the rocks, in fact they appear to have been the labourers, who were employed in addition to the masons or stone-squarers. All the artisans in Egypt were formed into Guilds or Companies, possessing " secrets " which were only revealed as the members progressed in their craft.

It is therefore not hazarding a guess to conclude that these barracks were inhabited by masons belonging to a guild, and that all the accurate squaring, levelling, dressing and polishing of the stones, which in its brilliant workmanship has never been equalled, was performed by them. These guilds had "a chief" and "a banner-bearer" and probably other officers. The chief kept a careful account of the workmen under him, noting down whether a member was "idle," or a "good worker," "religious," regular, ill, or even in one case that his wife and children were ill! The masons appear to have been vegetarians. There was, we are told, an inscription on the Great Pyramid, stating the amount of money spent on rations of "radishes, onions, and garlic," also we read of lentils and corn being supplied to another guild, resident in the City of the Dead at Thebes, which received in addition "jugs" of something or other, so probably these worthy masons were not total abstainers, unless indeed the jugs were the innocent receptacles of oil! The first "strike" on record occurred among the members of this Theban guild. The rations which were their due, did not come to hand, in fact the delay was so prolonged that they were on the point of starvation. They struck work, marched out in a body, and "crossing the five walls of the necropolis" demanded their due, "we have been driven here by hunger and thirst, we have no clothes, no food and no oil"! Provisions were sent down to them and they returned to the scene of their labours, however they seem to have got entirely out of hand for "the scribes and the two chiefs" argued with them but to no avail and finally the police and " the princes of the town " interfered. This exciting episode occurred under Rameses II., and we note that the company was "in residence " at their work, evidently the arrangements were similar to the immense barracks on the plateau at Gizeh.

Mention is frequently made of the " Three chiefs of the Stonemasons " who were always present to supervise difficult and elaborate operations. This is entirely in accord with the organisation of the Mediæval Guilds of Operative Free-Masons, at the head of which were Three Grand Masters who were the supreme rulers and final authority.

We may be sure that the pyramid barracks were the scene of many exciting episodes similar to those that occured at Thebes !

On the East of " the Great " was the temple, built of granite; it is now all in ruins, but two pieces of polished stone were found there both bearing the name of Khafra, proving that this king was really responsible for this pyramid and its temple, which is in accordance with the account of the ancient historians. A splendid built causeway runs diagonally from this temple to the Temple of the Sphinx, which lies South and rather East of that guardian of the Dead. Indeed many people, on quite insufficient grounds, have concluded that Khafra carved the Sphinx and built the Sphinx-Temple in addition to his own pyramid and its temple. That he was connected in some way with both is certain and it is more than probable that he excavated the Sphinx

from the sand which even in his day had engulfed
it. Nine statues of wonderful skill and obviously
living portraits of this King were found tossed down
a well in one of the Courts of the Temple of the
Sphinx. Only one has survived this rough treatment;
the figure is in a sitting posture and the face is
essentially that of a ruler of men, expressing strength
of will and dignity. In the utter destruction of
these portrait statues, coupled with the account that
this ruler also was feared and detested by the people,
lies further evidence that panic, more than political
enmity, was responsible for the smashing up of these
works of art. Fear gives rise to the most potent
form of hatred.

The name of the architect of these marvellous
structures has passed into oblivion, but the great
prince who was the "Superintendent of the Works"
of Khafra is well-known to us, and in imagination we
can join Prince Nebemakhet on his round of inspection of the pyramid, the temple, the statuary, and
the many other works undertaken by this active
king. He was accompanied in his duties by his
wife, and two long haired baboons followed them, to
the amusement of the masons who were entertained
by the gambols of these quaint pets.

Tradition narrates that in this pyramid ' there were
no less than thirty vaults full of marvellous treasure.
The secrets of science, malleable glass and " precious
iron that would twine about like cloth," the sacred
symbols of emerald, talismans of sapphire, annals
and histories, and images made with the substance
of the stars, to each star an image.'

The guardian of all this was calculated to inspire the stoutest heart with terror ; it was a rose granite statue, standing erect, a royal sceptre in its hand, and the uræus diadem upon its brow.

At the approach of any unlawful intruder, the uræus came to life, darted forward, curling round his neck in deathly coil, and having killed the wretch withdrew, and slept once more.

There was appointed to serve this guardian "an ugly deformed spirit which parted not from him."

There is some doubt as to the haunter of this pyramid, as the historians who narrate the Coptic traditions do not apportion the guardians, the servers and the haunting spirits, to the same pyramids, so in this case it may have been a Nubian, ancient of days, bearing a basket on his head and in his hands a thurible wherewith he incenses the statues and obelisks which were round about it.

These spirits could be propitiated by suitable offerings and sacrifices and then they were willing to reveal the secrets they so closely guarded, for "all these spirits are clearly seen by such as come near them. There are certain offerings for each, by means of which the treasures may appear, and that there may be friendship and familiarity between men and spirits," as the ancient author quaintly words it.

From Maspero.]
KHAFRA.

MEN-KAU-RA.

4.

" THE SUPREME."

"HERE were buried the Kings, the Masters of the Law, and the Priests, and by every priest his book and the miracle of his art and life."

IN due time Khafra "was gathered to his fathers " and Men-kau-ra reigned in his stead.

Whatever may be the differences of opinion regarding the characters of the two former kings everyone agrees that Men-kau-ra was a most exemplary ruler, devoted to the gods, and judging men with wisdom and mercy. Early in his reign he had the great misfortune to lose his only child, a daughter. Stricken with grief he determined that the obsequies should be in every way worthy of the exalted rank of the princess and royal heir. He caused therefore a heifer to be made of wood, hollow within, and richly ornamented with gold, with a globe of the same metal, glistening like the sun, between the horns, in this was reverently laid " the wanne and forlorne corpse of his best beloved daughter." This was sent to Saïs, and honoured with divine worship ; incense being offered at the shrine during the day, and a lamp burning before it at night.* But there was evidently a curse on this

* Herodotus, in this tale, describes the worship of Neith. How it was confused with Men-kau-ra's daughter it is difficult to understand !

King, no sooner had he recovered from this shock, than an Oracle gave forth the decree that at the end of six years he was to quit this mortal scene. Full of confidence in his righteous life and rule he was indignant at the seeming injustice of this verdict and sent a "reproachful message" to the Oracle explaining that his conduct contrasted well with his wicked predecessors who had oppressed the land ; that they had lived long, whereas he who was so clement and merciful was condemned to a speedy death !

The Oracle then proceeded to explain, that the most high gods had determined to afflict Egypt for 150 years, that the former kings knew this well and by their acts had but fulfilled the decree; whereas he, in his mildness and justice, was not obeying the behest of the gods, and so must die !

When Men-kau-ra heard this he knew it was final. He determined however that he would not be out-done and cheated of his lawful years, so he caused great illuminations to be made, and every night he spent " in exceeding great mirth and princely banquetings " while the day was filled with amuse-ments, sailing up and down the Nile, roaming in the woods and marshes and giving himself up entirely to pleasure. Thus by turning night into day he falsified the Oracle and spun out his allotted time to twelve years.

In the midst of this whirl of gaiety he found time to think of a pyramid* for himself. He called it

* The length of side is rather over 346 ft., and height is 215 ft., the casing is ¼ granite ¾ limestone.

"The Supreme" and it was to be of rose granite,
but alas! it was never finished and the upper part
was cased only with limestone. A wall encompasses
three sides, on the fourth, the East, there is a temple
approached by a causeway from the plain. The
site chosen was further South and more to the West
than the pyramids of his predecessors, and it is
oriented to the cardinal points, but unlike "The
Glory" and "The Great," it possesses two
entrances in the *centre* of the north face. The
upper apparently was the original one, terminating
on what was then the outside, but owing to the
enlargement and alteration of design it now lies far
back and is partially blocked up; the lower one is in
the fourth course. The name Men-kau-ra was carved
on the north side, we are told, but no casing-block
with the royal cartouche has ever been found; no
doubt it was torn off and is now broken up and
built into some obscure dwelling in Cairo!

The interior is most extraordinary and complicated.

Entering by the lower passage, it trends downwards through the granite masonry and afterwards
through the rock. The direction presently becomes
horizontal and then opens straight into the middle
of a room* and progresses beyond it—in fact this
room is more like two ample recesses on each side of
the passage, the walls are cut to resemble panelling,
and fragments of a sarcophagus were found in it.
In the passage beyond we come upon the sites of

* 10½ft. by nearly 13ft. by 4ft. high.

three gigantic granite portcullises, after the third the passage becomes much higher and passes into a fine lofty corridor or hall,* the length of which is at right angles to the passage. Gazing upwards we see high on the north wall just above the doorway, the orifice of another passage. This is the end of the original passage, already mentioned, which abutted on the face of the pyramid before the alterations were carried out. It is thought that at first it opened on to the floor of a vault, and that elaborate excavations were undertaken whereby the vault was turned into the present hall, but these extensive alterations resulted in the doorway being left up aloft (on the level of the former floor), so that a new passage was cut from the floor of the hall, outwards towards the North, terminating as we have seen on the fourth course of the pyramid. The old unused passage is at first horizontal and then slopes upward, it runs really above the new one; the lintel block over the original entrance is enormous, weighing about fifty tons.

On the north and south walls of the Hall are two pilasters, facing each other. They are placed on the west part of these walls and are so arranged that the breadth of each pilaster is equal to the width of the doorway ; from the edge of each to the west wall equals the space from the door jamb to the east wall ; from the further edge of each to the east wall equals the distance of the further door jamb to the west wall. This is really not so complicated as it seems !

* 46⅜ft. by 12⅔ by nearly 16ft. high.

Imagine two men in the hall one stationed at the extreme west end of the south wall, and the other at the extreme east end of the north wall. They start simultaneously to pace down the hall (in opposite directions naturally) ; as one reaches the pilaster the other arrives at the door jamb; next, the space being equal, the width of the pilaster and the width of the doorway are paced ; and finally the last lap, the longest, is also the same and the man reaches the extreme east of the south wall as the other one arrives at extreme west of the north wall ! It is an extraordinary method of spacing! Were the pilasters perhaps intended for doorways into other rooms ? The roof has an ornamented moulding just above them. Or is it perhaps designedly arranged thus, the pilasters being stations as it were, for some ceremony of circumambulation, round whatever object occupied the recess in the floor at that end of the hall.

This socket, or recess is cut into the floor to hold some object, not now there; it may well have been for the pedestal base of a portrait statue of Men-kau-ra, similar to the large basalt and diorite statues of Khafra.

When first entered, two objects of interest and value, were lying in this chamber, the basalt lid of a sarcophagus, and a coffin lid of cedar. On this wooden cover* is a text in hieroglyphics: " Hail, Osiris! King of the North and South, Men-kau-ra living for ever, born of heaven, conceived by Nut†

* Now in British Museum.
† Nut goddess of the sky.

offspring of Seb.* Thy mother Nut spreadeth herself over thee in her name of 'divine mystery.' She granteth that thou mayest exist as a god, without foes, O King of the North and South, Men-kau-ra, living for ever." Looking round for the coffers to which these covers belong we perceive another passage entrance! It goes straight down through the middle of the floor† in a westerly direction, sloping somewhat at first, but afterwards horizontal, and turning out of this passage, is still another! Neglecting this second in the meantime, but noting the holes in the walls which apparently at one time supported the ends of rollers over which the ropes passed for lowering (or hauling up) heavy weights, we pass westwards into the sepulchral chamber. It is cut out of the rock but is lined with granite throughout. The roof is particularly interesting as it exemplifies the principle of the arch, the sloping blocks support each other by thrust; the underside is then cut into a barrel vaulting making a pointed arch. The blocks for this granite ceiling were let down from the hall above, into the roof space in the rock, a short passage being cut for the purpose and then closed up.

Here, in this vaulted granite chamber was found a splendid blue basalt sarcophagus, cut from a single block, polished, panelled and ornamented to resemble a temple. Alas, it now lies at the

---

* Seb god of the earth.

† 17ft. from east wall.

bottom of the sea! Howard Vyse, overcoming insuperable difficulties in getting it out, had destined it for London, but the ship went down off the coast of Spain, and thus this work of art is lost to the world for ever!

The sarcophagus was empty when found. The Arabs said "The long blue vessel was empty." Yet scattered about on the floor were found the sad remains of a mummy, some yellow woollen cloth and some bundles of rags; also the same Arabs *did* find a mummy and some "golden tablets whereon was some writing that no man could read." It is very puzzling—the smashed sarcophagus in the panelled room, the empty one in the vault—the poor human remains—the tale of the mummy—from which coffer did it come?

Turning sadly from the sepulchral vault back into the passage we descend seven stairs going northward and east into what is called the Loculus Chamber, which lies 3 feet below the passage. This is the oldest known staircase in the world and it leads into a strange place! The door is in the south wall of a long chamber running diagonally, in the east are four narrow, deep recesses* and in the north wall are two more, these mysterious crypts are just adapted for sarcophagi and the arrangment for the rollers and ropes outside, looks as if much lowering had been anticipated,—but they are desolate and empty.

Opposite the staircase is a recess in the passage

---

* 8½ft. deep and about 2ft. 8in. wide at the entrance and not quite as high as the roof of the chamber.

wall for turning the sarcophagus as it was being taken in. There is plenty of room for many burials in this pyramid and there would need to be, as legend narrates it was destined to receive the "bodies of the Kings and the Masters of the Law and the Priests, and every priest his book and the miracle of his art and life"; and many wonders were there too, among them, a "laughing statue cut out of a green precious stone."

The firm belief that the "book" was buried with the priest, continually recurs, and Men-kau-ra will always be remembered in connection with two chapters in the *Book of the Dead*. It was in his reign that the "royal son Hor-dad-ef" set forth on his inspection of the Temples. During this round he made two wonderful discoveries: the "Chapter* of not letting the heart be driven away, in the under-world" was found "under the feet of a statue . . . . upon a slab of iron of the south in the time of His Majesty, the King of the North and of the South, Men-kau-ra, triumphant." It begins "My heart, my mother; my heart, my mother, my heart whereby I came into being," alluding to the belief that the heart was the definite cause of physical existence.

The other great discovery was the shortened version† of the magnificent "Chapter of coming forth by day in the underworld." It is a chapter of splendid beauty and will be remembered by the opening words, "I am Yesterday, To-day, and

---

* xxxb. Budge.

† lxiv. Budge. The long version is thought to date from the 1st Dynasty.

To-morrow, and I have the power to be born a second time." This was engraved on iron in letters of lapis lazuli and was also found by Hor-dad-ef.

The longer version was discovered some hundreds of years earlier by "the chief mason of the King."

The ownership of this pyramid is indeed difficult to determine. In spite of the name of Men-kau-ra being on the coffin lid there is evidence, equally valid, that this king was buried elsewhere. He apparently built another sepulchre for himself at Abu-roash ; he called it "The Beautiful." This second pyramid of his contains the fragments of a sarcophagus also of a diorite statue and of its base, and enough of a cartouche to suggest that it belonged to Men-kau-ra! This evidence is interesting in conjunction with the fact that "The Supreme" was not finished, and was then altered, and that Manetho avers that it belonged to Queen Nitaqerti of the VIth Dynasty, about 4100 B.C.

"Nitaqerti was the noblest and most beautiful woman of her age, fair in colour, and the builder of the third pyramid." Her throne name was Men-ka-ra, so probably confusion has arisen from the great similarity of the two names. Possibly Men-kau-ra did begin it but died before its completion and was buried in "The Beautiful," then in years yet-to-come, Nitaqerti Men-ka-ra finished it, altering the interior plan, and was duly buried therein, anyhow her place of sepulture has not been found.

Nitaqerti means "The Rosy One," and the Greeks catching at the meaning, identified her with their " Rosy One," the courtezan Rhodopis of later times.

It is in relation to the Rosy One that we first hear the story that is known to Western children as " Cinderella and the Slipper." As the Rosy One was bathing in the river an eagle pounced on one of her golden sandals, and bearing it away let it fall into the lap of the king who was sitting in judgment at the court in Memphis. He sought out the owner of the dainty sandal and made her a queen— history does not confirm this legend !

All the confusion has arisen over the meaning of the word and many authorities say that " The Rosy One " was not a person at all, but really the rose one, *i.e.*, the red granite pyramid !

Nitaqerti, the beautiful queen, had a tragic life. Her husband and brother were cruelly murdered by the nobles of the court. Her mode of avenging their death was unique. She constructed a magnificent subterranean building and invited the aristocracy of Egypt to a banquet at the opening ceremony. When the feasting was at its height and the gaiety and the music resounded through the hall, she silently withdrew and opened the sluices of a concealed canal, and then locked the doors. The revelry disguised the rushing of the waters until it was too late ; there was no escape, the princes and the hereditary lords of Egypt were drowned and her husband was avenged ! But her own life was at an end and killing herself, she found her last resting place in the " Supreme."

This pyramid was guarded by a small image of

" eagle " stone (from the enchanted City of the Black Eagle, now engulfed in the sands of the Sahara) on a base of the same stone, which statue drew towards it the awestruck intruder until he stuck to it, so that he could not move and finally he went mad or died !

There was also a spirit appointed to serve it, which " parted not from it."

This guardian can only be explained by a dynamo or by hypnotism; the attraction, the adhesion, the paralysis cannot otherwise be accounted for.

In a pyramid that is so inextricably complicated with legends of a great queen it need cause no surprise that the spirit that haunts it always appears in " the form of a woman of extreme beauty; with an enchanting smile she draws men to her, and when they are distracted with love, laughs at them so that their senses leave them and they become mad with love and grief. Divers persons have seen her walking about the pyramid at noon and sunset."

5.

MISCELLANEOUS PYRAMIDS.

THE trio of small pyramids built for Khufu's family rank next to his own in masonic skill. They lie beyond it, to the East. In their construction a new feature was introduced, the lines of junction of the faces were edged with diorite and basalt, the hard black stone contrasting effectively with the white casing. Of course all of them have been ransacked and rifled. The first, the most northern of the three, was originally lined with small squared white stone, and a plain blue basalt sarcophagus was found smashed up in it. The middle one has always been ascribed to Henutsen, Khufu's daughter, about whom the Saïte dragomans told such scurrilous tales. After the spoliation it appears to have been used as a general cemetery, for many skulls were found there, but among the *débris* a small hand, a woman's, of brown stone, much worn, was discovered—all that is left, perhaps, of the statue of Henutsen.

South of Men-kau-ra's pyramid there is another trio of smaller ones, one of which is so much larger than its fellows as actually to be sometimes alluded to as the Fourth Pyramid, thus including it among the famous three.

Tradition says that the three wives of the three

famous Kings Khufu, Khafra, and Men-kau-ra, were buried in these tombs.

In the largest, in a plain granite coffer, was found the mummy of a young woman with remarkably fine teeth, and in the roof, in red paint, the cartouche of Men-ka-ra. This presents a further complication to the problem of confusion between the King Men-kau-ra of Dynasty IV. and the Queen Men-ka-ra (Nit-aqer-ti) of Dynasty VI.—*Who* does this cartouche allude to ? Was the queen buried here, instead of sleeping her eternal sleep in the blue sarcophagus in the upper chamber of " The Supreme"? The wanton destruction of the robber of all ages has probably removed all chance of ever solving the problem.

The Arabs say there is an underground passage from this one, to Men-kau-ra's pyramid. The whole ground seems rammified with subterranean chambers and passages, crossing and re-crossing and leading hither and thither, a veritable labyrinth.

At the top of the walls, the border has been purposely cut away all round, it was undoubtedly engraved. One fragment alone is left on which are the words " giving life."

Before leaving the subject of pyramids the " pyramid of degrees " and the pyramid of Unas must be mentioned.

The former has no less than four entrances that we know of; it is a perfect catacomb of passages and rooms and in the lowest there is a secret chamber to which access is obtained by removing a four ton stopper in the floor ! The main hall is 77 feet high ! A great deal of wood has been used in the interior of this pyramid so possibly the disproportionate height is caused by the floorings of the upper stories having given way. One of the vaults has been lined with greenish blue, glazed porcelain tiles, and the ceiling was decorated with stars on a blue ground.

The pyramid of Unas* is also at Sakkara and has several chambers. The sepulchral vault is lined with alabaster and covered with inscriptions which are as fresh and brilliant as when completed. How the artist contrived to paint in the dark remains a mystery, but one of the "marvels" of this ancient race was that "even in the great obscurity of the night people saw clearly without torches"!

Long texts from the *Book of the Dead* adorn the walls, and we find here the first affirmation of the profound belief in the immortality of the soul and in the life after death :—

"O Unas, thou hast not gone dying but thou hast gone living to Osiris."

* 4308, B.C.

II.

THE LABYRINTH.

" It surpasses even the pyramids."

AMONG the many Egyptian buildings that were celebrated in classical writings, none is more remarkable in its effect upon the imagination than the famous Labyrinth.

At the mere mention of the word, the vivid picture arises of Theseus and his adventures; how with the clue, bestowed on him by Ariadne, he set forth in search of the terrible monster, the Minotaur, and how after much wandering his trials were crowned with success.   But whatever other charms the Egyptian labyrinth may have had, it lacked a Minotaur!   It is well-known that Dædalus, the Cretan architect, took the design from Egypt when commanded by Minos to construct the Labyrinth.   It is even thought that the word itself is a corruption of good Egyptian for Laprohunt " the palace by the canal," others again think it is from λαβρυς the double axe, for the great palace in Crete was the 'house of the double axe' and had this device on the pillars.   As the building and probably the name were derived from Egypt, perhaps also the strange story of the wanderings, and the monster to be triumphed over, are also the garbled fragments of some ancient allegorical ceremonial which took place in the intricate windings of the original labyrinth.

Like pyramids, this form of building seems to belong to ancient races that preceded the Aryan.

The Etruscans possessed both pyramids and labyrinths, and in that extraordinary monument which was said to be the tomb of Lars Porsenna the pyramid and the labyrinth were joined in a geometrical plan which included the square and the circle.

" He was buried without the city (Clusium) under a monument of squared stones ; each side was 300 feet broad and 50 feet high. Within the square base an inextricable labyrinth had been constructed, whither whosoever adventured, without a clue, could not find a passage out. Upon this square were placed five pyramids, four in the angles and one in the centre, 95 feet broad at the bottom and 150 in height. The tops were connected with a circle from which bells were suspended by chains, rung by the wind as at Dodona. Upon this circle four other pyramids and above this five more."

This extraordinary sepulchre has disappeared but there is a somewhat similar tomb labyrinth at Albano where Aruns his son was buried.

At Lemnos there was another labyrinth famous for its pillars ; it had no less than 150 columns in it. Ruined and forgotton are the Etruscan tombs. The Cretan obtained an adventitious interest from the terrible Dweller, the Minotaur that haunted its winding passages, but the locality of the building can no longer be identified at all, and the Egyptian, older than any of them, for centuries was known only from legend ; so absolutely had all its glories passed away that even its site was unknown !

All accounts agreed that it was in the Fayoum and lay beside the canal in full view of all the boats sailing up and down from the Nile to Arsinoë—in spite of this circumstantial evidence of its position not a trace apparently remained, and yet it was a puzzle how any building so enormous and so famous could absolutely disappear.

The Fayoum was the favourite resting place of the sovereigns of the XIIth Dynasty.

They had made of it a fertile and beautiful land. At the entrance stood a town, "The Repose of Senusert,"—could any name more adequately describe how these kings regarded the district ?

It was adorned with pyramids and temples, and two colossal statues of brilliant quartzite rose from the lake and scintillated in the dazzling sun. Amenemhat III. in stone thus watched over the work of his brain and of his hands. He was buried at Hawâra in a fine pyramid which overlooked the entire extent of the land he loved. Adjoining the pyramid was found an immense area of ruin, and as we know the Labyrinth was by the canal, and as there is nothing else in the vicinity which can compare with this site, we may decide that at last, after so many ages, it has revealed itself! The foundations are 1,000ft. long and 800ft. broad, thus covering an area that vindicates the opinion of the ancients when they said it "surpasses even the pyramids."

Lately the mounds of rubbish have been cleared away; a sordid little brick village of Roman date occupied the Temple site, when the celebrated structure was destroyed and made into a quarry for the buildings of the conquerors! The classic authors vaguely indicate that the arrangement and number of the halls corresponded to the divisions of Egypt; that in fact the Labyrinth was a central depôt where everything appertaining to the government, the people, and the country, was synthesised. There is no certainty, for the accounts are fragmentary; Strabo says there were twenty-seven halls, Herodotus tells of twelve courts, six facing north and six south, but the number of the Nomes of Egypt appear to have varied from time to time. The methods of division no doubt were different for different purposes; our counties and parliamentary and postal divisions by no means correspond and probably they had similar arrangements. The foundations indicate that part at least, of the building was a peristyle Temple. A great central hall with two crossways can be traced. Opening out, on each side of the first crossway, are courts or small temples. The second crossway is a pillared hall with courts on one side only. Herodotus tells us that each court was surrounded with a colonnade of white stone and that the walls were covered with sculptured figures. The building was of two stories, and each contained 1,500 rooms, the total being 3,000! He revelled in the beauty of the upper portion, the rooms he says " presented a thousand occasions of wonder," and he passed in bewilderment from courts to " rooms, and from rooms to halls, and to other corridors from the halls, and to other courts from the rooms "; but the lower portions he did not visit, the Egyptians " would on no account show them because there were the sepulchres of the Kings who originally built this Labyrinth " ! Who really built it and what its purpose, is a secret not yet disclosed. Part of it at least was built about 3400 B.C. by Amenemhat III. and part by his daughter Sebekneferu who came to the throne later. Of this Queen little or nothing now is known, a grey sphinx, a few columns, a scarab seal and this cylinder of white schist

CYLINDER OF QUEEN SEBEKNEFERU, B.C. 3300.

[*British Museum.*]

beautifully glazed with blue and bearing her royal titles, are all that remain ; and yet in the great work of constructing the Labyrinth we know she played as important a part as Amenemhat, and her name was inscribed on the stately pillars which adorned the building !

It contained many treasures of value inestimable. One, which no doubt adorned the great peristyle temple, was a colossal statue of Serapis thirteen and a half feet high, carved out of an emerald of great price !

III.

THE SPHINX.

"THE Lion-god with awesome eye."

Nesi-Khonsu.

ON the confines of the desert, gazing eternally into space, rests the Sphinx, colossal, enigmatic, and of immemorial age. Carven out of the living rock, the massive lion-body and human head, form one of the most remarkable monuments in this land of wonders.

What its age and who made it, remain undiscovered, but the purpose can be surmised from its position and from its strange composite nature of man and beast.

The Egyptians were adepts in representing weird nondescript creatures. Many of them, in later ages were no doubt symbolic; some of them may have had an astronomic import, and others perhaps were traditional memories, the echoes of primeval days, when, as geology has shewn us, the world was really inhabited by gigantic monsters of strange form.

To the imaginative, the mysterious desert was, perhaps, still the habitat of similar prodigies; and so we find in their hunting scenes, among ordinary

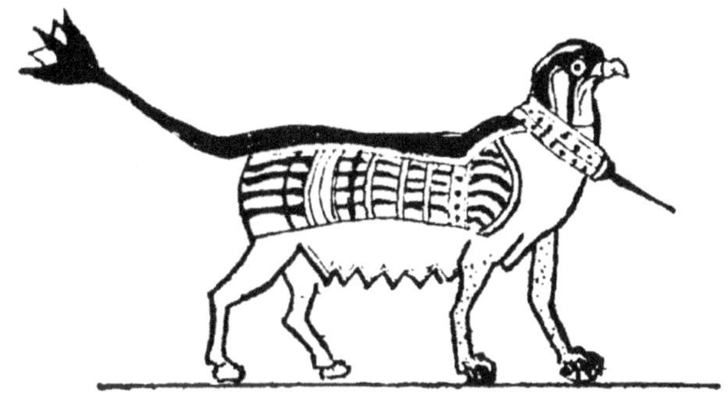

The Sag

The Setcha

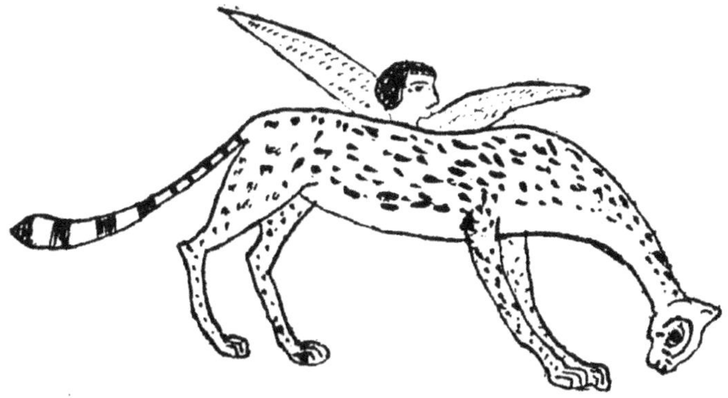

After Wilkinson.]

THE HUMAN LEOPARD.

E. Wedgwood

"HU," THE SPHINX

wild animals, fabulous leopards with the head and neck of a serpent, or a panther with a winged human head on its back, or that delightful animal the Sag, whose tail terminated in a lotus blossom, half horse, half lion with the head of a hawk, and yet which was obviously tame as it wears an ornate collar !

Surely these were representations of swiftness, strength, and cunning, over which man gained the mastery. On the other hand, the strange lions, with giraffe's necks, found on the pre-dynastic slate palette of Nar-Mer (made to celebrate a victory more than 7,000 years ago !) are distinctly heraldic in grouping, and may have had a stellar significance.

Many of the gods, too, are represented with heads of animals, especially the hawk and the lion. This was no doubt a symbolic representation of the divine attributes or functions, and also referred to the position of the equinoxes and solstices in the zodiacal constellations at different epochs. This particular mode has been carried on well into modern times and provides us with examples that illustrate and interpret the more ancient custom. The vision of Ezekiel, the strange phraseology of " The Revelation of St. John the Divine " and the animals that were both the emblems and types of the four Evangelists, belong to the same ancient form of symbolism, while the astronomical application is seen in the phrase " the Lamb of God " and " Christ is that Fish."

The serious creation of chimerical monsters seems then to have been either a vestige of ancestral memory and tradition, or a symbolic representation of divine attributes, or an astronomic method of indicating periods of time. The Sphinx undoubtedly is a similar conception emanating from the same type of mind and belonging to one or other of these three categories. It is essentially the product of Egypt, although to-day it goes by the Greek name Σφιγξ, and it has no connection, or likeness in any way with that winged she-monster of riddle-propounding fame, the idea of which was undoubtedly borrowed, in later ages, from its inscrutable Egyptian prototype.

In Egypt the creature has always the body of a lion, generally in the position which in Heraldry is designated couchant. The head varies and although generally that of a man, ram-headed specimens are well known and a hawk-headed variety is occasionally seen.

But the Sphinx, *par excellence*, is the man-headed lion resting in the desert sand at Gizeh. Rock-hewn and of titanic proportions it forms an impressive and commanding statue even in this land of colossal sculpture. The body is about 150 feet long, the paws giving an additional 50 feet; the head rears itself 70 feet on high, and is 30 feet long, the face being about 14 feet wide. The neck gives the impression of being too slender to support so massive a head, but this is only because the lower portion of the head-dress has fallen away. Originally the face was painted red and upon the brow rested the Uræus, the symbol of royalty and divinity. The features have been much damaged

during the last few centuries and the colouring is
nearly gone, but nothing alters the wonderful eyes
expressing dignity, strength and calmness.

A pathway between the paws leads to a little
temple or shrine which stood against the breast.
Formerly a wide and magnificent staircase descended
to this. From the level there was a descent of
thirteen steps to a platform on which stood a small
building, then a stairway of noble proportions—
thirty steps—led down to an altar, which stood in
front of the outer court of the temple, and just at the
tip of the monster's paws. The entrance was behind
this, so that the temple court lay between the paws.
Advancing, we reach the shrine, the doorway of
which was guarded by a lion, couchant and facing
the Sphinx. The little temple consisted of three
walls and had no roof. The eastern wall is the
famous stele of Tahutimes IV., recording how he had
repaired the statue of the God and cleared away the
devastating sand, and mentioning that Khafra had
also engaged himself in some similar work—but
what, is unfortunately obliterated. This is one of
the very few allusions to the image by the Egyptians,
and the only one of incontestable date. The north
and south walls were stelae of Rameses II. The
whole three originally may have occupied the Great
Temple, having been dedicated as offerings to the God.
They are much older than the constructions round
them and were probably removed after the temple
fell into ruins and used to erect the shrine in later
times, for the staircase and buildings are of late
date.

This stele of Tahutimes shows the Sphinx couchant on a pedestal which is itself a building. It walls have an architectural ornament recessed, and there is in the centre an immense doorway. It would be interesting to have the entire area deeply excavated to see if this representation was based on reality.

The Temple of the Sphinx is alluded to by ancient authors and generally it is considered to be the temple in which Khafra's statues were found and which many think that Khafra built—there is room for doubt and if the building depicted on the stele is a copy of what existed, the Temple of the Sphinx remains still undiscovered.

There are several interesting references by the Greek and Arab writers who, coming in later days, recorded their impressions of the greatness and the antiquity of this monument.

Pliny's remarks are so full of significance, especially the first few sentences, that we give the passage in full.

"In front of these pyramids is the Sphinx, a still more wondrous object of art, but one upon which silence has been observed, as it is looked upon as a divinity by the people of the neighbourhood. It is their belief that Harmais was buried in it, and they will have it that it was brought there from a distance. The truth is, however, that it was hewn from the solid rock; and from a feeling of veneration, the face of the monster is coloured red. The circumference of the head, measured round the forehead, is 102 feet, the length of the feet being 143, and

STELE OF TAHUTIMES.
(From Lepsius Denkmäler.)

the height from the belly to the summit of the asp on the head sixty-two."*

Here is suggested a possible explanation of the strange reserve of the Egyptians concerning so awe-inspiring a subject. The next point is remarkable, the tradition† that, gigantic as it is, the Sphinx had been brought from afar and erected on its present site; of course Pliny is incredulous, and states the undoubted fact that it is carved out of the solid rock. But the two ideas are by no means inconsistent, and in Egypt such wonderful works had been accomplished in the same line, that if the sand had not been cleared all round below the absolute base level, it would have been impossible to negative even such an amazing tradition as is here recorded.

The engineering skill displayed by this race in the manipulation of colossal masses of stone, borders on the miraculous. The beautiful rose granite statue of Rameses II. weighs 900 tons; it was brought from quarries 150 miles distant. Amenhotep III. erected two statues of himself weighing 800 and 1000 tons respectively.

What these were like, can be judged from the colossal head of this monarch, which now smiles benignly over the pigmies hurrying backwards and forwards in the Egyptian gallery of the British Museum! But all these, gigantic as they are, fade into insignificance beside the shrine‡ at Buto, in the

* *Hist. Nat.* xxxvi. 17.

† A similar tradition states that Stonehenge was transported from Ireland by the magic arts of Merlin.

‡ Here, the "living Uraeus" was worshipped under the form of a Goddess.

Delta. Herodotus describes it as made from one single stone, the external surface of which formed a perfect cube of 75 feet in height, length, and breadth. The weight has been estimated at between 5,000 and 6,000 tons, it is of red granite and the nearest quarries of this stone are at Aswân, the other end of Egypt! Considering the accomplishment of this project it would be rash to dismiss the tradition of the transport of the Sphinx on the ground of impossibility!

"Harmais* was buried in it," Pliny artlessly repeats. The region of the West belonged essentially to the dead; pyramids, walled temples, and tombs innumerable, lay round about. Here, too, in the West, was the entrance of that path mysterious, which leads from this world to the next, and Harmais, the Sun-god, dying daily, descended also into the West, at his nightly setting—therefore was he, in one sense, truly "buried there."

Beyond this Kingdom of the Dead, lay the desert, the abode of strange beasts and frequented by the "children of the serpent Apep, the impious ones who haunt the solitary places and the deserts." The whole district was under a spell, hostile and invisible potencies came out of the desolate waste and again vanished through "the door eternally ajar"; apparitions and spectres wandered in the neighbourhood, bringing madness and death to the unfortunate man who beheld them. Realising

---

* Harmais, Harmachis, the Greek attempt at the Egyptian word Hor-em-khuti, Horus of the two horizons, a form of the Sun-god.

the panic of the wilderness, the wayfarer sought with relief the " sacred way," at the foot of the hill, which led finally to safety and to Memphis. The fear inspired by this ghost-ridden locality has lasted until to-day, and the lord of the district, the Sphinx, became the Father of Terror.

Abd-al-Latîf, in his brilliant description* of Egypt in the thirteenth century, indicates the true reason why all mention of this monument was avoided.

" About a bow-shot from these pyramids a man may see the colossal figure of a head and neck emerging from the ground. To this figure the name of ' Abu'l-hawl ' (*i.e.* Father of Terror) has been given, and it is said that the body to which this head belongs is buried under the ground. Judging of the dimensions of the body by that of the head it must be more than 70 cubits in length. The face is red-coloured, and on it is a red varnish, which is as brilliant as if it was new. This figure is very beautiful, and its mouth bears the impress of grace and beauty, and it may be said to smile graciously."

Turning now to the ancient Scriptures much light is thrown on the symbolism and function of the Sphinx. The *rôle* of the lion was always pro-tection, therefore the Sphinx was the guardian and the protector.

The Egyptians called it "Hu," and to them it was the emblem and image of the God " Horus of the two Horizons," a form of Rā whose symbol was the sun. In that sublime hymn "*The seventy-five*

* De Sacy's Translation.

praises of Rā," the double sphinx-god is mentioned ; " Praise be to thee, O Rā, exalted Power, thou art the double sphinx-god . . . thou art the Lord of Light and declarest the things that are hidden." Obviously, in this connection, 'declarest' means to make manifest, but the lion is also used as a symbol for the unmanifest, the "hidden god," Amen, whose name even "is hidden," and then the lion is always couchant on a pedestal.

In the *Book of the Dead* we find the lions seated back to back, or (heraldically expressed) sejant and addorsed, supporting the disc of the Sun which rests on the horizon. In this position, facing East and West, they guard the gates of morning and of evening and therefore are they appropriately named " Yesterday" and "To-day." The relation of the unity to the duality, is expressed in the text " Thou wast the Lion-god, of the twin lion-gods." The one, being Amen Rā, the Sun-god; the dual, being phases of the Sun, or other dualities that arise when one becomes two. In most instances this duality indicates pairs of opposites ; the two horizons, East and West, marking the rising and the setting sun, morning and evening, yesterday and to-day.

In the following illustration the idea is further amplified, being applied in a more abstract manner, the physical night and day, light and darkness, carrying the moral significance of good and evil. Thus, in the *Book of Pylons,* we find a strange sphinx, inhabiting the Ninth Division of the Underworld. It has the head of a hawk, which is surmounted by the white crown of Upper Egypt, standing erect upon its back is a dual-headed image of Horus-Set. A verse from another portion of the ancient Scriptures explains this: " The double Lion-god hath founded thy habitation. . . . Horus purifieth and Set strengthens, and Set purifieth and Horus strengthens."*

Horus and Set being combined into one figure, the idea of good and evil is presented as equally divine twin aspects of the One. The whole conception is carried into the next world, giving a further duality of this life and the next.

Useful as was protection to the living, it was even more essential to the dead, hence the presence of the sphinx in the underworld. The strange and beautiful book, entitled "*The beginning of the horn of the West, the remote boundary of solid darkness,*" describes the extreme end of the Underworld and the descent of God into Hell; in the midst thereof is the " hidden land of Seker," and we find it guarded by two sphinxes !

Affording protection in both worlds, the sphinx also superintended the new birth : " I am the child of yesterday, the twin Lion-gods have made me to come into being."†

The firm belief, therefore, in the efficacy of the protective power of the lion was seen by the lion-form of the bier, " the bier which giveth life,"‡ on which the Egyptian slept his eternal sleep ; therefore too was the great Sphinx placed at the entrance

* *Book of the Dead*, Chap. xvii., Budge.
† *Book of the Dead*, Chap. lxiv., Budge.
‡ *Book of the Dead*, Chap. lxiv., Budge.

of that path on which each man must walk alone; and so we still find it to-day, fronting the rising sun, on its face a faint smile, inscrutable and yet benign, ever keeping watch and ward over the mighty city of the dead, which lies at its feet.

What evidence is there as to its age? There is nothing satisfactory, for so far, we only find *two* mentions of it in the ancient historical records of thousands of years; so chary was this nation of uttering the Name of that which was regarded both with veneration and awe!

In the little temple near one of the small pyramids was found the tablet of Pa-seb-khanu of the XXIst Dynasty,* this implies that Khufu had seen the Sphinx. The tablet itself is of very inferior workmanship and belongs to the same era as the temple in which it was found, but the question arises, was it a copy of an older record? It does not profess to be so and its contents are distinctly of a much later age, but it at least shews that there was a tradition that the Sphinx was in existence before the time of Khufu and that this monarch chose the spot for his pyramid because it was already sanctified by the presence of that colossal statue and by the Temples of Isis to the north and Osiris to the south of it.

On the stele of †Tahutimes IV., 1423 B.C., Khafra is named, but as a portion of the inscription is destroyed it is very uncertain whether that Pharaoh was mentioned as the maker. In the so-called

---

* 1076 B.C.

† The Greek form Thothmes is frequently used.

Temple of the Sphinx the only statues that have been found are of that king, but he may have repaired and added to it when he was undertaking such immense building operations on the site, though it is more probable that he merely cleared away the sand from both the Sphinx and the temple.

In the middle of the back of the lion is a tomb shaft; not much can be argued from this, it may have been made in a later age when the Sphinx was no longer reverenced, or it may have been sunk much earlier before the solid rock was carved out at all, and the casing stones would hide it when the work was complete.

We can therefore safely assume that this great monument is certainly not later than Khafra 4685 B.C. but in nature it is so entirely archaic that probably it was very old even in his day.

In the XVIIIth Dynasty the sands had accumulated round it to a great extent. Tahutimes the young prince was " practising a spear-throwing for his pleasure " and hunting in the neighbourhood. When " the hour came in which he granted rest to his servants," he took advantage of it to offer up seeds of flowers, and prayers, to " Horus of the two horizons " for, " a great enchantment rests on this place from the beginning of time . . . because the form of the Sphinx is a likeness of . . . . . the very great God who abides at this place, the greatest of all spirits, the most venerable being who rests upon it." He then " stretched himself to rest in the shade of this great God and sleep overtook him." He dreamt in his slumber that

Hor-em-khu came and spoke to him "as a father speaks to a son," and after promising him that he will succeed to the throne and have a long, happy, and successful reign, proceeds thus, " the sand of the district in which I have my existence has covered me up. Promise me that thou wilt do what I wish in my heart: then I shall know whether thou art my son and my helper" . . . here the inscription is defaced, but " he understood the words of the God and laid them up in his heart," and later, when he ascended the throne, he cleared off the sand and built a shrine between the paws, whereon is inscribed this story !

From historical sources nothing more definite can be obtained than the certainty that it was in existence in the reign of Tahutimes IV., and the implication that Khafra had either made it or cleared away the sand that perpetually obliterated it.

But there is another way of approaching the subject, and we can fall back on the zodiacal application of the animal chosen as type, and attempt thus to arrive at a definite era, through a consideration of the lion symbolism as an astronomic method of dating. Observation and comparison shew that this works well, when applied to other religion-indicating symbols,* and this gives us confidence to proceed in the same manner in the case of faiths more ancient and more obscure.

---

* The Christian symbols of the lamb and the fish point to the passing of the vernal equinox from Aries to Pisces, from this we deduce that the Christian religion arose about A.D.—and this is right.

First, four points must be settled. Are we to base our calculations on equinoxes or solstices; and when that is arranged, from which of the four quarters,—the choice lies between the vernal equinox, the summer solstice, the autumnal equinox and the winter solstice, occurring in the constellation Leo.

Fortunately we are relieved from anything so destructive to accuracy as guesswork or speculation !

A chance remark in the classics* gives us a clue: "The keys of Egyptian Temples bore the figure of a lion, from which chains were suspended having a heart attached to them," and further, the explanation is volunteered, that this alluded to the Inundation occurring when the Sun was in the constellation of Leo. This quotation is also of considerable interest to students of Astrology, for they aver that each constellation of the Zodiac has a portion of the human body assigned to it, and that Leo governs the heart. The *Book of the Dead* contains several remarkable confirmations of that theory.

The Chapter of " Not letting the heart be carried away in the Underworld "† begins with the invocation " Hail, thou Lion-god "; and furthermore another text states " The double Lion-god . . . hath established my heart through his own great and

---

* The *Scholiast* of Arātus, about 270 B.C.—he wrote an astronomical poem.

Plutarch also says that the Temple doors were ornamented with "the gaping jaws of the lion."

† Chap. xxviii., Budge's translation.

exceeding strength."* But to return from this fascinating by-path to the point at issue—when did the Inundation occur in Leo? The Nile always begins to rise in June, so the basis of calculation is settled and the question is merely, when did the summer solstice fall in Leo?

Nowadays the summer solstice falls, in reality, in the *constellation* of Gemini (about the end of it), although according to the modern system of nomenclature it is in the *sign* Cancer. Bearing in mind the Precession of the Equinoxes, it is obvious that 6000 years intervene between to-day and the era required, therefore the summer solstice occurred in the constellation of Leo about 4000 B.C. Comparing the result of this calculation with the known facts, we find that this date cannot be right.

All authorities agree that the Sphinx existed in the time of Khafra. Khafra lived nearly 700 years before this time, so 4650 B.C. is the very latest date we can assign to this monument, and many would place its erection here. Others, noting the archaic style and giving weight to the popular opinion expressed in Pa-seb-khanu's tablet that Khufu saw the Sphinx, consider that Khafra only repaired it and that it belonged to an earlier date. But it is more than probable that there was, however, at this time, a revival of the old form of lion-worship and a restoration of the ancient monuments, and many of the classic allusions† to the Lion-Goddess would possibly refer to this era.

* Chap. lxxviii., Budge's translation.
† Mycenæan, Cretan and Pelasgian.

We must therefore relinquish this date, of 4000 B.C. and follow the revolutions of the Zodiac backwards for another cycle. Again the summer solstice fell in Leo 25,800 odd years before, *viz.*, about 29800 B.C. The bare suggestion of the possibility of such a date will incur the scorn of the orthodox and may strain the credulity even of the credulous! But after all, the classic authors acknowledge that the Egyptians possessed observations of total eclipses of the sun and moon, going back 20,000 years, and they themselves claimed records extending even further back, so perhaps the date proposed is not after all so impossible as at first glance it appears. But it is one thing to propound a theory and quite another to prove it! We acknowledge that no absolute proof is at present possible, but we would like to draw attention to the much neglected and belittled records of the Divine Dynasties. From these, several interesting points of information can be drawn, that confirm the suggestion and turn it into an acceptable and reasonable hypothesis, until time offers definite proof.

The account of the Divine Dynasties contains an interesting combination of factors; a study of Cosmogenesis, the story of the creation of the Solar System; and the setting-in-order of this world told in an allegorical and dramatic manner which lends itself also to a symbolic interpretation; the legendary history of the Divine Kings and a consecutive account of the development of religion, art and science, under them.

But no student of these records can seriously

doubt that running through them all, are fragments of real history, immensely ancient :—strange stories of early reigns, of a golden age of happiness and peace ; of famines and pestilences laying waste the land ; of floods devastating the world ; of colossal wars deluging the country with blood ; and many other incidents, long forgotten, surviving only in these old-world rumours ; the echoes of Kings who in the night of time ruled Egypt.

In the Second Divine Dynasty a period of hostility and strife convulsed the kingdom. It began with a rebellion but the malcontents afterwards joined forces with the followers of Set, so that a terrible and prolonged war ensued.

" In the year 363 of Horemkhuti, the King of the South and North, who liveth for ever and ever, his Majesty found himself in the country of Nubia . . . because certain folk had conspired against their lord." He put down the rebellion but later, the revolt again breaking out, he deputed his son Horbehudtet to take command of the army. The war raged up and down the Nile valley. The rebels, aided by Set, opposed themselves to the Egyptian forces both by land and sea, but under the brilliant leadership of Horbehudtet they were defeated at Thebes, Denderah and Tanis, the remnants of the vanquished enemy escaping finally into the mountains and by the Mediterranean.

Having disentangled these strands of fact from the myth, and remembering that Horemkhuti is always represented as the man-lion, the Sphinx, we note that during these wars the Prince Horbehudtet also " took the form of a lion," and thus obtained victory on several occasions. After one triumph, too, the name " Great Protector " was bestowed on him.

To celebrate the conquest of his enemies Horemkhuti " ordered that statues of himself should be set up."

Is the Sphinx one of these statues?

Perhaps on the death of this Divine Ruler of ancient times, this monument was really erected to commemorate his life and reign, in which case Pliny was right when he said, " Harmais is buried there."

To us, the Mystery of the Sphinx is still undisclosed, though dimly guessed at ; perchance, in some future age, the magic insight of archæology may lay bare its hidden secret ; and reveal still further " the profound and mysterious knowledge of Egypt, containing the arcana of Greek antiquities, the key of many obscurities and ancient learning extant."

NARMER'S PALETTE MONSTERS.
(From a cast in Edwards' Collection.)

LONDON :
WOMEN'S PRINTING SOCIETY, LTD.
BRICK STREET, PICCADILLY.